En parejas 1

A Four–Book Series of Communicative Activities

Lucía Caycedo Garner
University of Wisconsin—Madison

Debbie Rusch
Boston College

Marcela Domínguez
University of California, Los Angeles

Houghton Mifflin Company   Boston

Dallas   Geneva, Illinois   Palo Alto   Princeton, New Jersey

Illustrations by Walt Fournier
Activities 5, 8, 10, 11, 14, 18, 19, 20, 22, 24

Illustrations by Stephanie O'Shaughnessy
Activities 6, 9, 13, 15, 16, 21

Photographs
Activity 9: AP / Wide World Photos

Cover design by Darci Mehall

ISBN: 0–395–55428–4

Library of Congress Catalog Card Number: 90–83013

BCDEFGHIJ-B-9987654321

Contents

Actividad 6: Haciendo planes

Communicative functions

Making plans . Stating obligations . Expressing likes and dislikes . Getting information from a newspaper listing . Negotiating

Language focus

Ir a + *infinitive* . **Gustar** . **Tener que** + *infinitive* . Simple present

Topics and vocabulary

Verbs . Time expressions . Question words: **dónde, cuándo, a qué hora** . Stem-changing verbs **querer** and **poder** . Days of the week

Actividad 7: La agenda

Communicative functions

Getting and giving personal information about schedules . Filling out a calendar . Making suggestions

Language focus

Ir a + *infinitive* . Question formation . Simple present . **Debes** + *infinitive*

Topics and vocabulary

Days of the week . Time expressions . Question words: **cuándo, a qué hora**

Actividad 8: El accidente

Communicative functions

Describing people . Asking for clarification . Requesting assistance

Language focus

Simple present . Adjective agreement . Either/or questions . **Ser**

Topics and vocabulary

Adjectives . Question words: **cómo, qué**

Actividad 9: ¿Quién es?

Communicative functions

Asking about people . Asking for clarification

Language focus

Ser . Question formation (either/or, yes/no) . Simple present

Topics and vocabulary

Verbs . Adjectives . Occupations . Parts of the body . Physical characteristics

Actividad 10: La universidad

Communicative functions

Describing and asking about location

Language focus

Simple present . **Estar** + *place* . Question formation

Topics and vocabulary

Prepositions of location . Places . **¿Dónde?**

Actividad 11: Encuentra las siete diferencias

Communicative functions

Describing actions in progress

Language focus

Present progressive . Reflexive and non-reflexive verbs

Topics and vocabulary

Everyday actions . Beach vocabulary

Actividad 12: El crucigrama

Communicative functions

Giving and understanding definitions

Language focus

Ser para + *infinitive* · **Estar** + *preposition of location*

Topics and vocabulary

Parts of the body · Clothing

Actividad 13: Se perdió

Communicative functions

Describing appearance · Asking for clarification

Language focus

Ser · **Tener** · Question formation · Adjective agreement

Topics and vocabulary

Physical characteristics · Adjectives · Colors · Clothing

Actividad 14: Si te doy esto . . .

Communicative functions

Describing clothes · Negotiating an exchange

Language focus

Ser (de) · **Llevar** · **Tener** · Indirect object pronouns

Topics and vocabulary

Clothing · Colors · Adjectives · Materials · **Me gustaría**

Actividad 15: ¿Cómo es tu familia?

Communicative functions

Describing family members · Asking for specific information

Language focus

Tener + *age* · Simple present · Question formation

Topics and vocabulary

Family members · Occupations · Age

Actividad 16: El catálogo

Communicative functions

Ordering from a catalogue · Taking an order

Language focus

Question formation · Simple present

Topics and vocabulary

Clothing · Colors · Numbers · Sizes

Actividad 17: ¿Es igual o diferente?

Communicative functions

Describing objects · Understanding descriptions

Language focus

Ser de + *material* · **Ser para** + *infinitive* · Passive **se**

Topics and vocabulary

Materials · Verbs · Household objects

Actividad 18: El mensaje telefónico

Communicative functions

Giving and receiving a message · Telling someone what to do

Language focus

Tener que + *infinitive* · **Ir a** + *infinitive* · **Deber** + *infinitive* · Simple present

Topics and vocabulary

Verbs · Days of the week · Time expressions

Actividad 19: ¿Quién vive en qué piso?

Communicative functions

Problem solving . Sharing information

Language focus

Simple present

Topics and vocabulary

Prepositions of location . Ordinal numbers . Nationalities . School subjects

Actividad 20: Ordenando el cuento

Communicative functions

Telling and sequencing a story

Language focus

Simple present . **Hay** . Preterit

Topics and vocabulary

Verbs (regular and irregular)

Actividad 21: ¿Qué más necesitamos?

Communicative functions

Discussing food needs . Sharing information

Language focus

Tener que + *infinitive*

Topics and vocabulary

Food . Measurements

Actividad 22: ¿Lo hizo?

Communicative functions

Discussing what chores have been done and what needs to be done

Language focus

Preterit . Question formation . **Tener que** + *infinitive*

Topics and vocabulary

Verbs (regular and irregular) . Rooms in a house . Common household objects . **Ya / todavía**

Actividad 23: Hispanos famosos

Communicative functions

Exchanging information about famous Hispanics

Language focus

Preterit . Question formation

Topics and vocabulary

Verbs (regular and irregular) . Dates . Occupations . Nationalities

Actividad 24: Las últimas vacaciones

Communicative functions

Describing past activities . Discussing future plans . Expressing preferences

Language focus

Preterit . **Tener que** + *infinitive* . **Ir a** + *infinitive*

Topics and vocabulary

Verbs (regular and irregular) . Places . Question words (review) . **Me gustaría**

Actividad 25: Amigos

Communicative functions

Describing people . Expressing likes and dislikes

Language focus

Simple present

Topics and vocabulary

Physical appearance . Sports . Personal information

To the Instructor

En parejas is a four-book series of communicative activities designed to supplement the first two years of a college or university Spanish program or all four years of a high-school program. The underlying premise of the series is that students learn best by doing. *En parejas* offers elementary and intermediate students of Spanish interesting communicative activities that provide realistic practice of important language functions. The information gap format, in which pairs of students perform tasks simultaneously on the basis of differing information, increases student communication time and provides a natural motivation for speaking. These activities provide an important support for achieving effective student-to-student interaction.

Description of the Series

Each book is divided into two sections: the first part for student A and the second part, which is upside down, for student B. Each student has a different set of information needed to carry out a task; for example, when making reservations, student A has a train schedule and student B has a description of the destination and times he/she must inquire about. The instructions for each student are separated in order to create the information gap.

The activities in each book practice the high-frequency functions, grammar points, and vocabulary covered in most texts. The use of pair activities decreases student anxiety and increases speaking time, thereby providing an environment that is conducive to language learning. This is in keeping with the goals of the oral proficiency movement and current trends in language teaching.

How to Use En parejas

Student Responsibilities

In order to receive the maximum benefit from the use of pair activities, encourage students to have fun and to use their imagination. They should know that they are active participants in their own learning process and that, during pairwork, they have the following responsibilities:

1. to work cooperatively.

2. to look only at their own information and not to peek at their partner's book.

3. to enunciate and speak clearly and to insist on clear pronunciation from their partner.

4. to ask for clarification if needed.

5. to correct each other's grammar when necessary.

6. to use their hands to gesture unless specifically instructed otherwise.

Once students recognize their responsibilities during pair work, anxiety will decrease and a productive environment will be established.

Selecting an Activity

En parejas is intended to enhance classroom teaching. The activities are designed to be used either as culminating activities after studying a particular function, grammar point or word set, or as reentry of already learned items. Students should already have worked with and should be familiar with the structures and vocabulary needed to carry out the task. The activities are not meant to be used during the introductory or drill phase of instruction. If students are well-prepared before doing an activity, errors should be minimal and should not impede communication.

Although the order of activities is in keeping with the sequences commonly presented in many textbooks, the activities may be done in any order as dictated by the course syllabus and the judgment of the instructor. The table of contents indicates which functions, grammar points, and vocabulary are needed to carry out each activity. Consult the table of contents to choose activities that are appropriate for the topic being covered in the classroom. High-frequency functions are practiced more than once, allowing the students to apply their knowledge to a variety of situations.

Forming Pairs

Vary partners frequently so that students are constantly working with different members of the class. Here are a few suggestions for forming pairs:

1. Pair students according to ability: stronger students with weaker ones or strong with strong.

2. Pair students randomly:

    a. Divide the class in half and have students number off; then number 1 works with number 1, number 2 with number 2, etc.

    b. Students choose their partner themselves.

    c. Arrange students alphabetically: pair students from opposite ends of the alphabet or according to the class roster.

3. Arrange groups by sex: males with males or males with females.

For classes with an odd number of students, have one group of three students work together with two of the students doubling up to work one part; have one student monitor a pair of students; or, place three students who work quickly in one group, thus allowing them to do the activity twice.

It is not recommended that you pair yourself with the extra student, since you should monitor all groups, answer any questions that come up, and make sure that all students are on task and actively engaged.

Many of the activities in the series simulate real-life situations. In order to help students visualize the scene, have them recreate the situation as much as possible. For example, when simulating a phone conversation, students can sit back to back. Or, if recreating a scene in a store, one student can stand behind his/her desk, which represents a counter.

Introducing an Activity

Before beginning an activity, make sure students understand the function or functions being practiced and the grammar and vocabulary needed to carry out the functions. Pay special attention to the useful expressions that are given at the beginning of each activity.

To ensure that each student knows exactly what his/her role is, read through the directions with the students or have the students read through the directions alone. Circulate at the beginning of the activity to make sure all students are working appropriately on the task. It is also possible to model the beginning of an activity with a student or to have two students model the activity before having the whole class begin.

In order to ensure that all students become involved immediately, set a time limit on the activity. Students will attack the task with more vigor if the time limit is a little bit less than what actually may be needed. For example, if an activity should take approximately seven minutes, set a time limit of five minutes. Since some activities are open-ended, it is important for students to know how much time they have.

If a follow-up activity is going to be done (such as reporting back to the class with your findings, writing a newspaper article about the person you are interviewing, etc.), make sure this is clear before beginning.

While an Activity Is in Progress

It is important to monitor pair activities. At this time you may do any or all of the following things:

1. Make sure students are on task.

2. Offer suggestions.

3. Answer questions.

4. Correct individual errors when communication is impeded.

5. Note grammatical errors for further classroom work.

6. Note problem areas of pronunciation for further classroom work.

While an activity is in progress, you must decide when to stop the activity. It is not necessary that all groups finish each activity. Just playing the game can be more important than winning. When two or three groups have finished, they can either reverse roles or you can end the activity for the whole class.

Wrapping Up an Activity

No matter how you choose to end an activity, it is important that the students know how they will be held accountable for what is accomplished during the pair activity. Here are a few suggestions for wrap-up activities:

1. Have individuals report their findings to the class. The first activity in each book allows students to get to know each other. A group sharing at this point may be quite productive to reduce anxiety.

2. Identify a group that has done something humorous and have them share with their peers, either by reporting back or by acting out the activity for the class.

3. Many activities can be self-checked by having pairs compare their completed activity (pictures, lists, data, etc.).

4. Collect and correct for accuracy activities that require a specific interchange of data.

5. Assign a brief composition, newspaper article, follow-up letter, etc., based on the contents of the activity.

Advantages of Pairwork

Frequent use of interactive pairwork activities provides a variety of benefits, including the following:

1. Students learn to depend on and learn from each other through cooperative interaction.

2. Self-esteem is fostered: every student is important and vital to the interaction.

3. Student motivation increases since every student must participate in the activity.

4. Class dynamics improve.

5. As students gain confidence in their abilities, their fear of speaking decreases and motivation increases.

6. Individual creativity and imagination are encouraged.

7. Problem-solving skills are strengthened.

8. The foreign language becomes a natural means to convey real meaning and personal ideas.

9. Students learn to have fun and express humor in Spanish.

10. The language learning process becomes enjoyable and self-directed.

To the Instructor

En parejas 1

ESTUDIANTE A

Actividad 1:   La inscripción

Fill out the following card with information about yourself.

Primer apellido

Segundo apellido

Nombre

Edad

Ciudad natal

Estado

Número de teléfono

En caso de emergencia llamar a:

Primer apellido

Segundo apellido

Nombre

Número de teléfono

Parentesco: —— Padre   —— Madre

                  —— Otro/a   (especifique relación _____)

You are a student helping with registration at your school. Ask the student who is registering questions to complete the following card. Since this is a conversation between two young people, you will address your partner in a familiar manner. When you are finished, switch roles. Ask questions like:

¿Cómo te llamas?
¿Cuál es tu número de teléfono?
¿Cómo se escribe . . . ?

You begin by saying: *Buenos días. ¿Cómo te llamas?*

Primer apellido

Segundo apellido

Nombre

Edad

Ciudad natal

Estado

Número de teléfono

En caso de emergencia llamar a:

Primer apellido

Segundo apellido

Nombre

Número de teléfono

Parentesco: _____ **Padre**   _____ **Madre**

_____ **Otro/a**   (especifique relación _____)

Actividad 2: Información, buenos días

Your boss asked you to call directory assistance to get the phone numbers of the following people. Jot down the phone numbers in the memo you will give to your boss. Use the following expressions to obtain the information you want from the operator:

Quisiera el número de teléfono de . . .
¿Me puede decir el número de teléfono de . . . ?

Your partner will begin.

MEMO

Carlos:
Necesito el número de teléfono de las siguientes personas: Peter Andersen, Paulina Peres, Miguel Jiménez o Giménez (no sé si es con "J" o con "G" pero vive en la calle Lope de Rueda), y Bibiana Domínguez Turrión.
Gracias,
José

Memo

José:
Aquí tienes los números de teléfono:

Peter Andersen: _____ _____
_____ _____
_____
_____

Atentamente,
Carlos

Actividad 3: Estación del Norte

You work at the information desk at the train station. Student B calls you for information about arrival times. Answer his/her questions, using the following information.

You begin by answering the phone and saying: *Estación del Norte, buenos días*.

L L E G A D A S		
PROCEDENCIA	*HORA*	*ANDÉN*
Salamanca	9:35	5
Zamora	10:05	8
León	10:30	3
Oviedo	Retraso 11:45	2
Santiago	12:40	6
Vigo	Retraso	

You are responsible for the travel arrangements for your company's sales representatives in Caracas. You have to check on the status of the flights for the following employees who should be leaving today. The airport has been having problems due to a pilot strike. You need to find out the departure times and the gate numbers so you call airport information. Use the following phrases:

¿Sabe Ud. . . . ?
¿De qué puerta . . . ?
¿Hay retraso?
¿Me puede decir a qué hora sale . . . ?

Your partner will begin.

					Hora	Puerta
Roberta Morales	Pan Am	632	Miami		_____	_____
Carmen Rey	Lan Chile	301	Santiago		_____	_____
Wilson Lerma	Iberia	465	Madrid		_____	_____
Víctor Malatesta	Avianca	345	Bogotá		_____	_____
Jesús Coello	Lacsa	203	San José		_____	_____

Ask your partner questions to complete the following weather map for Argentina. Exchange information. Use expressions such as:

¿Qué tiempo va a hacer mañana en . . . ?
Mañana va a hacer . . .
Va a estar . . .
Va a . . .
Va a hacer . . . grados.

You begin by asking: ***¿Qué tiempo va a hacer en Mar del Plata mañana?***

Actividad 6:   Haciendo planes

You want to go out with your friend to the movies this week. Ask your friend what his/her plans for the week are and decide which film you would like to see. Use the following partial list of movies in your city and your work schedule to help you make your decision. Useful expressions include:

¿Qué vas a hacer el martes?	**Tengo que . . .**
¿Tienes planes para el jueves?	**No me gustan . . .**
¿Estás libre el miércoles?	**¿A qué hora . . . ?**
¿Quieres ver . . . ?	**No puedo, necesito . . .**

You begin by saying: *¿Quieres ir al cine conmigo esta semana?*

■■■ *Cartelera para esta semana* ■■■

CINESTUDIO 1
Rainman   drama con Tom Cruise y Dustin Hoffman, mayores de 18 años. 7:10, 9:15, 11:20.

CINESTUDIO 2
Martes 13 parte V   terror, mayores de 18 años. 7:00, 9:00, 11:00.

GOYA
¿Quién engañó a Roger Rabbit?   comedia: mayores de 13 años. 4:45, 6:50, 8:55, 11:00.

GRAN VÍA
Psicosis   suspenso, mayores de 18 años. 7:00, 9:05, 11:10.

METROPOLITANO
Bambi / Blanca Nieves y los 7 enanitos   dibujos animados de Disney, todas las edades. Viernes y sábado 4:30, 7:30.

Horario de trabajo

lunes: __6:00 pm a 12:00 pm__

martes: __libre__

miércoles: __6:00 pm a 12:00 pm__

jueves: __6:00 pm a 12:00 pm__

viernes: __libre__

sábado: __2:00 pm a 8:30 pm__

domingo: __2:00 pm a 10:00 pm__

Actividad 7: La agenda

You are talking to your new business partner on the telephone and are trying to get information about his/her plans for the week. You both have just started a company that distributes sports equipment. You need this information because you think he/she has not been working as hard as you have lately, and you want to be prepared should a confrontation be necessary in the future. Fill out the following calendar with your partner's schedule.

You know he/she will be traveling on business. If he/she goes to any of the following cities you would like him/her to do some specific things for you:

Use phrases like:

Necesito saber tus planes para esta semana. ¿Qué vas a hacer el lunes por la mañana?

¿Vas a . . . ?

Debes . . .

Your partner will begin.

Copiapó: Vender raquetas de tenis a la tienda Tres Gatos

Valparaíso: Hablar con 1340 AM sobre anuncios comerciales en la radio

Valdivia: Vender bicicletas a la tienda Ciclimundo

Punta Arenas: Hablar con el agente de Rafael Serma (el futbolista)

lunes: _____
_____

martes: _____
_____

miércoles: _____
_____

jueves: _____
_____

viernes: _____
_____

sábado: _____
_____

domingo: _____
_____

You have just returned from taking your parents to the bus station. They are leaving Santa Marta and going to Cartagena for a vacation. They will be departing at 3:30. You receive a phone call informing you that your uncle has had a serious accident and is in the hospital. You have to call the bus station and page your parents to stop them from leaving. You may need to say:

Es una emergencia. Tengo que hablar con mis padres.

Your partner will begin.

Tus padres

Actividad 9:   ¿Quién es?

Your partner is thinking of a well-known living or fictitious person. Your job is to ask him/her questions to determine who this person is. You may want to determine physical appearance, age, occupation, where he/she lives, etc. Your partner can only respond by saying **sí** or **no**. When you have guessed the identity, switch roles. Repeat as many times as you like. Here is a list of famous people for your partner to guess:

1. Meryll Streep

2. Barbara Bush

3. Perry Mason

4. Vilma Picapiedras

5. Eddie Murphy

6. Magic Johnson

7. ???

You may want to make a game of this by awarding a point for each question asked. The person who determines the correct identities while asking the least number of questions is the winner.

You begin by saying: *¿Es mujer?   ¿Es político / actor / etc.?   ¿Es joven?*

You are at the Universidad Cristóbal Colón and you need to find out the location of the following places: **el parque de las esculturas, la facultad de matemáticas, el cine, el laboratorio de idiomas**. Ask your partner questions such as:

¿Sabes dónde está . . . ?
¿El parque está . . . ?

Your partner will begin.

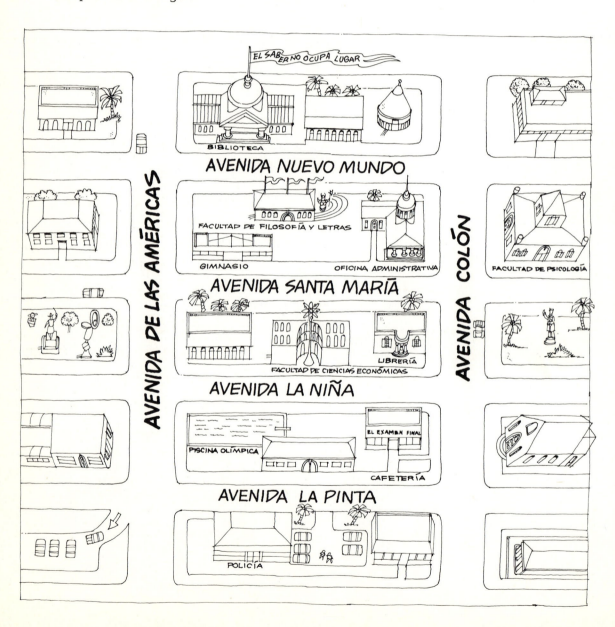

Actividad 11: Encuentra las siete diferencias

You and your partner have a similar but somewhat different drawing. There are seven differences between them. Describe your picture and ask questions about your partner's picture to find out what the differences are.

You begin by saying: *Hay un hombre joven que está quitándose la camiseta.*

The following crossword puzzle is on clothing and parts of the body. You have the vertical words and your partner has the horizontal ones. You need to give clues **(pistas)** to your partner. Use phrases like the following:

> **Es generalmente de . . .**
> **Esta parte del cuerpo está en . . .**
> **Es para . . .**

When your partner is finished, you will ask him/her for clues about the horizontal words.

Your partner will begin.

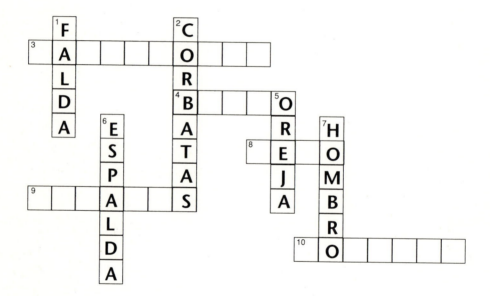

Actividad 13: **Se perdió . . .**

You have lost your grandma in a department store and you go to the store manager to see if he/she can help you. Describe your grandma to him/her. Use phrases like:

Es gorda / delgada / alta.
Tiene pelo . . .
Tiene . . . años.
Lleva . . .

You begin by saying: *No sé dónde está mi abuela.*

Actividad 14:   Si te doy esto . . .

You have an identical twin sister who lives in Salta, Argentina, where it is usually hot. You live in Tierra Del Fuego, Argentina, where it is very cold. You will be taking a trip to the Dominican Republic to enjoy the beaches. Make a list of what you think you will need and call your twin sister to see if you can borrow some clothes. In the past you have always lent each other clothes, but neither of you ever gives the other anything without getting something in return. Use phrases like: **Voy a ir a . . . Necesito . . .   Me gustaría tener . . .   Si me das . . . te doy . . .**

Other vocabulary that may be helpful: **de rayas   de lunares   de cuadros**

Your sister will begin.

This is your family tree (you are the person circled in black). You want to find out the names, occupations, and ages of your partner's family members. You will have to ask very specific questions. Try to reproduce his/her entire family tree. When you are finished, your partner will ask you questions about your family to reproduce your family tree. Don't volunteer any information that is not specifically asked of you. You begin by asking questions like:

¿Cómo se llama tu padre?   **¿Qué hace tu hermano?**
¿Cuántos hermanos tienes?   **¿Cuántos años . . . ?**

You begin by saying: *Hola, ¿cómo te llamas?*

Flora Vegas,
ama de casa, 87 años

Javier Dávila,
ingeniero, 89 años

Berta Roca,
dentista, 50 años

Javier,
médico, 52 años

Manuel,
abogado,
45 años

Adriana Muñoz Morales,
artista, 42 años

Laura,
economista,
25 años

Lorenzo,
estudiante,
20 años

Dani, artista, 25 años

You are in Puerto Rico at a workshop and you need to buy some summer clothing since you are planning on staying an extra week to enjoy the island. Your budget is $175. Here is a page of a catalogue from Tienda Los Gallegos. Call the store to place a phone order. You are in a hurry and are making this phone call during a break.

Your partner will begin.

Tu tarjeta de crédito:

BANCO HISPANO

VISA

3245 9803 8749 8374

Fecha de Vencimiento 10/96

P. MONTERO TEDIAS

tienda ▪ los ▪ gallegos

(809) 798-6549

Si lo pide hoy, lo recibe mañana antes de las 10:00 a.m. o le devolvemos el dinero.

TRAJE DE BAÑO

La mejor manera de conocer a una mujer es llevar un perro a la playa.

Talla: pequeña, mediana, grande

Color: negro con perros blancos, blanco con perros negros

Precio: $34.69

BIKINI

Perfecto para tomar el sol en la playa

Talla: pequeña, mediana, grande

Color: azul marino con lunares amarillos, negro con lunares blancos, blanco con lunares negros

Precio: $39.75

CAMISETAS

Camisetas de rugby de manga corta, unisex para personas activas

Talla: pequeña, mediana, grande

Color: azul con rayas verdes, rojo con rayas amarillas

Precio: $44.99

SOMBRERO HARRISON FORD

Sombrero para hombres o mujeres en busca de aventuras

Talla: pequeña, mediana, grande

Color: beige

Precio: $29.79

TOALLAS

Toallas para la playa

Color: anaranjado con rayas amarillas, azul claro con dibujos de Disney, rojo con rayas blancas

Precio: $15.99
Dos toallas: $29.99
Tres toallas: $42.95

PANTALONES CORTOS

Para la persona moderna, unisex, pantalones cortos con diseños geométricos

Talla: pequeña, mediana, grande

Color: negro con el diseño en blanco, blanco con el diseño en negro

Precio: $42.39

Actividad 17: ¿Es igual o diferente?

You have to describe to your partner the odd-numbered objects in your list without actually saying the word. Your partner will describe to you the even-numbered objects. On hearing your partner's descriptions, you have to decide if he/she is describing the same object you have under the same number.

You begin by saying: *Es algo que se usa para . . .*

		Iguales	Diferentes			Iguales	Diferentes
1.	diccionario	____	____	6.	jabón	____	____
2.	cuchillo	____	____	7.	computadora	____	____
3.	champú	____	____	8.	lámpara	____	____
4.	maleta	____	____	9.	tenedor	____	____
5.	cama	____	____	10.	televisor	____	____

You work as a receptionist at Turitur, a travel agency. Here's a memo from your boss, Mrs. Rey, with messages for some of her clients. Someone calls for her but she is not in, so you have to take a message and check whether there is a message for this caller.

You begin by answering the phone: **Turitur, buenos días.**

De: Marta Rey

A: Paulina

Tengo que salir ahora pero vuelvo dentro de dos horas. Aquí hay mensajes para algunos de mis clientes. Para <u>Carola Olmos</u>: ya está confirmado su vuelo a Costa Rica. Es el vuelo de LACSA 420 que sale el viernes 4 a las 2:15 am.
Para <u>Mariano Mores</u>: el precio de la oferta a Cancún, México, subió. Ahora cuesta $250 por persona. Hay vuelos a Cancún los domingos por la tarde y hay vuelos desde Cancún todos los fines de semana.
Para <u>Sandro Ortega</u>: debe pagar su pasaje antes del jueves próximo porque el pasaje va a subir. Puede pagar con tarjeta o con dinero en efectivo. Los vuelos más económicos son los vuelos de los lunes y martes por la mañana.

MR

MENSAJE TELEFÓNICO

Para: _____

De parte de: _____

Teléfono: _____

Motivo de la llamada: _____

_____

Recibido por:	Fecha:	Hora:

Actividad 19: ¿Quién vive en qué piso?

Look at the drawing of the student residence below. Share your clues (**pistas**) with your partner to complete the chart on the next page. Here are some useful expressions:

¿Puedes repetir, por favor?   **¿Dónde vive . . . ?**
No entiendo.   **¿Qué estudia . . . ?**

Your partner will begin.

1. Carmen Quesada vive en el último piso y estudia ingeniería.
2. El chico que vive en el último piso es de Bolivia.
3. Tomás Schaeffer, de Chile, vive en el 4º A.
4. La chica que vive justo debajo de Pablo es mexicana.
5. La estudiante que vive al lado de Carlos estudia química.
6. Jorge Martinelli, estudiante de guitarra, es del país que está al lado de Chile.
7. La chica que vive en el 2º A estudia educación.
8. Carlos López, que estudia matemáticas, vive en el apartamento A, al lado de Sonia Rodríguez.
9. Marta Menéndez, que vive al lado de Gustavo, estudia computación.

Nombre	Nacionalidad	Estudiante de . . .	Apartamento

Actividad 20: Ordenando el cuento

The following pictures are part of a story and, except for the first one, they are out of order. Your partner also has drawings that are part of this story. Ask your partner about the pictures he/she has, to find out the order in which the events happened. When you finish putting the drawings in order, give the story a title. Use expressions such as:

¿Qué ocurrió después?
¿Tienes un dibujo de la chica en un accidente?

You begin by saying: ***En el primer dibujo hay . . .***

Actividad 21:   ¿Qué más necesitamos?

You and your friend are planning a meal for tonight at your friend's place. Each of you has a recipe as well as a picture with some ingredients that you have at home. Find out what ingredients neither of you have, so that you can stop at the supermarket on the way to his/her house.

Your partner will begin.

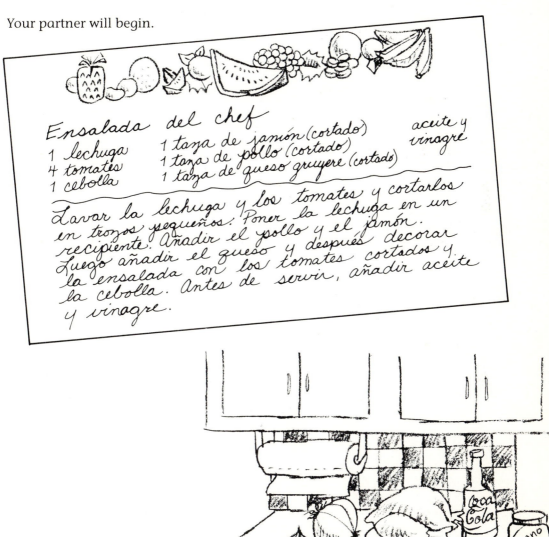

Ensalada del chef

1 lechuga   1 taza de jamón (cortado)   aceite y
4 tomates   1 taza de pollo (cortado)   vinagre
1 cebolla   1 taza de queso gruyere (cortado)

Lavar la lechuga y los tomates y cortarlos en trozos pequeños. Poner la lechuga en un recipiente. Añadir el pollo y el jamón. Luego añadir el queso y después decorar la ensalada con los tomates cortados y la cebolla. Antes de servir, añadir aceite y vinagre.

Actividad 22: ¿Lo hizo?

You and your roommate are having a party tonight at your apartment. Your mother has been visiting and has offered to do the cleaning. You are out running errands and you call your roommate to check on what your mother has done. Ask your roommate about the things from the following list you need to have done. Ask questions using the preterit.

Your partner will begin.

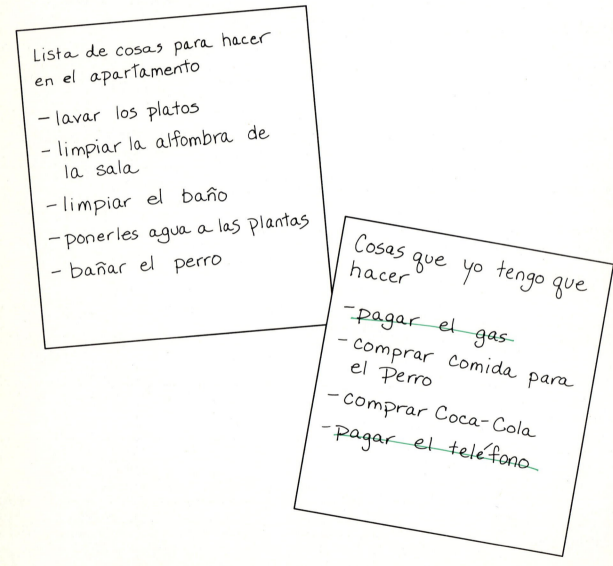

Lista de cosas para hacer en el apartamento

- lavar los platos
- limpiar la alfombra de la sala
- limpiar el baño
- ponerles agua a las plantas
- bañar el perro

Cosas que yo tengo que hacer

- ~~Pagar el gas~~
- comprar comida para el perro
- comprar Coca-Cola
- ~~Pagar el teléfono~~

Actividad 23:   Hispanos famosos

Complete this chart about famous Hispanics by asking your partner questions. Make sure to use the preterit when exchanging information.

You begin by saying: *¿En qué año nació Frida Kahlo?*

	FECHA	NACIONALIDAD	OCUPACIÓN	ALGO IMPORTANTE
Frida Kahlo	? – 1954	mexicana	pintora	
Salvador Allende	1908 – ?	chileno	político, presidente de Chile, médico	nacionalizar las minas de cobre
Pablo Casals	1876 – 1973	español	violoncelista, director de orquesta	empezar el Festival Casals en Puerto Rico
Alfonsina Storni	1892 – 1938	argentina	poetisa	
Emiliano Zapata	? – 1919	mexicano	político revolucionario	
Isabel la Católica		española	reina	
José Martí	1853 – ?	cubano	poeta, escritor, abogado	escribir la letra de *Guantanamera,* padre de la independencia de Cuba.
Carlos Gardel	1887 – 1935	argentino	cantante, compositor	
Violeta Parra		chilena	cantante, compositora	empezar la Nueva Canción chilena
Roberto Clemente		puertorriqueño	jugador de béisbol	morir en un accidente de avión llevando comida y medicina a Centroamérica

Actividad 24: Las últimas vacaciones

Ask your partner about his/her last vacation. Ask specific questions. Try to use all of the following question words and phrases.

¿Adónde . . . ?   ¿Por qué . . . ?
¿Cuándo . . . ?   ¿Cuánto dinero . . . ?
¿Con quién . . . ?   ¿En qué hotel . . . ?
¿Cuánto tiempo . . . ?   ¿En qué restaurantes . . . ?
¿Qué . . . ?   ¿Qué souvenirs . . . ?

When you are finished, your partner will ask you about your last vacation. Base your answers on these pages from your scrapbook.

	Fecha de salida	Hora de salida	Hora de llegada
Mazatlán/ México	14/12	5:59 AM	10:45 PM

¡TACO LOCO!

Restaurante económico

Yo ♥ Mazatlán

**HOTEL CAMINO REAL
MAZATLÁN, MÉXICO**

La salsa

Comida típica

2 HABITACIONES DOBLES

7 NOCHES $350.000

After discussing your vacations, plan a trip together, taking into consideration each other's likes and dislikes. Use phrases such as:

Me gustaría . . .   Tenemos que ir a . . .
Podemos ir a . . .   No quiero . . .
Debemos visitar . . .   ¿Por qué no vamos a . . . ?

Actividad 25: Amigos

By this time you should know most of the people in your Spanish class quite well. Write a description of one of your classmates on the card below. It should be a minimum of ten lines. Make sure your clues go from general characteristics to more specific ones. When you are finished, read the description to your partner to see if he/she can guess who it is. Then your partner will read his/her description. Use phrases such as:

> **Es una persona alta / baja / delgada / etc.**
> **Tiene pelo . . .**
> **Tiene . . . hermanos / años.**
> **Le gusta . . .**
> **Vive en . . .**
> **Juega al . . .**

You begin by saying: **Es una persona . . .**

NOTAS NOTAS NOTAS NOTAS NOTAS NOTAS NOTAS NOTAS NOTAS NOTAS

NOTAS NOTAS NOTAS NOTAS NOTAS NOTAS NOTAS NOTAS NOTAS NOTAS NOTAS NOTAS NOTAS NOTAS

NOTAS NOTAS NOTAS NOTAS NOTAS NOTAS NOTAS NOTAS NOTAS NOTAS NOTAS NOTAS NOTAS NOTAS

NOTAS NOTAS NOTAS NOTAS NOTAS NOTAS NOTAS NOTAS NOTAS NOTAS